A Return to the Stars

MY HOME

Ashtara

with

The Arcturians, Mary, a Magdalen
and Djwhal Khul (D.K.)

Copyright © 2025 Ashtara

Published by Tara Rising Press.
www.tararisingpress.com

Prepublication Data available from the National Library of Australia

ISBN: 978-0-9803178-5-5 (pbk)
Also available as an ebook
Ebook ISBN: 978-0-9803178-8-6

All rights reserved. No part of this book may be reproduced or transmitted in any form or by any means, electronic, or mechanical, without written permission from the author or publisher, except for quotations embodied in critical articles or reviews.

Cover design: Janene Grigg
www.in2artdesigns.com

Book design and publishing assistance by
Publicious Pty Ltd.
www.publicious.com.au

DEDICATION

To all conscious and self-aware individuals who
have experienced the light and love of the Divine
Mother Goddess, and who seek to enlighten
others to experience the same vibration.

May your lives be blessed and your inner
light continue to shine brightly.

Also written by Ashtara

Gaia, Our Precious Planet

Tara, Emissary of Light

The Great Cosmic Joke

A Treasure Trove of Gems

A Crack in the Cosmic Window

Your Recipe for Empowerment through Spiritual Astrology: Volumes One, Two and Three

Esoteric Astrology: The Astrology of the Soul

Arcturus Astrology: A Consciousness Accelerator for the Aquarian Age

I am an Experiment: An Extraordinary Spiritual Adventure

The Magdalen Codes: Reclaiming Ancient Wisdom

A Story Never, Ever Told: A Reveal.

For more information, please visit www.ashtara.com

GRATITUDE

This book I share was guided by my long-term spiritual guides, the Arcturians, Mary, a Magdalen and Djwhal Khul (D.K.). Through their love, my life has totally transformed into a joyful expression of truth. Their clear transmissions form the main part of this book.

During one early morning in February 2023, I received an unusual telepathic transmission from the Arcturians, light beings from the star system of Arcturus, a lighter realm than that of planet Earth. Their message came in the form of an invitation to the readers of my weekly newsletter, Cosmic Currents. Having worked with the Arcturians since 1997, when they transmitted an earlier book, Gaia, Our Precious Planet, and having shared their regular messages with my readers for many years, I trust their methods.

This particular transmission was an invitation to readers to support me and my work. Astounded by the number of readers who answered their call, and with immense gratitude, I thank my Mission Camelot team for their love, support and practical assistance.

From all over the world, these wonderful people answered the invitation. Danielle Helms, Ian Davies, Amery Burleigh, Shayne Hertzberg, Jennifer Trevalyn, Kristin Tyson,

Deborah Lovegrove, Louise Fewtrell, Mary Hardwick, Angela Haldane, Christine Seed, Patricia Schultz, Ruth Bryant, Judith Clarke, Fiona Glover, Alejandra Lopez Carpio, Mary Meyer, Bronwyn Baird, Jan Jervis and Julie Burnett. I thank you all from the bottom of my heart.

Together we have a mission to accomplish and we will do so.

We have been on amazing adventures together, with many more to follow. Telepathically guided by the Arcturians and Mary, a Magdalen, we are working on developing a spiritual mission dedicated to the Children of Light and the creation of a world where harmony, beauty, wisdom and truth reign supreme.

A special thank you to Dr. Jan Jervis, PhD, for her overall guidance with the formatting and design of this book, Christine Seed for her editing, Louise Fewtrell for her spiritual guidance and Jennifer Trevalyn for her unique talents in working behind the scenes to assist not only its production but also future ones.

Through your loving support, this book will aid and accelerate the development of our sacred mission.

To Janene Grigg (www.in2artdesigns.com) for creating the book cover image. Upon my request for a book cover that symbolised a new world forming, she created the amazing cover. Thank you Janene.

CONTENT

PREFACE Ashtara i

Introduction iii
    SERPENTS OF WISDOM xiii

Part One: Ascension
    ASCENSION 1
    SECOND ASCENSION 4
    A THREE-FOLD SPIRITUAL FLAME 12
    A LONG HIDDEN TRUTH REVEALED 14
    A NEW LIFE IN A NEW LOCATION 16
    THE ARCTURIAN'S REQUEST 25
    METAPHOR, SYMBOLS AND ARCHETYPES 27
    JOURNEY TO FRANCE 35
    MULTI-DIMENSIONAL VIEWING 41

Part Two: A Continuation
    A CONTINUATION. A Story, Never,
    Ever Told. A Reveal 45
    THE BAR 50

A NEW CREATION	56
THE COLLEGE OF COSMIC CONSCIOUSNESS	58
A LONG LIFE LIVED	64
THE LIGHT OF DAWN	66
THE LIFE OF A SOUL	70
AFTERWORD	73

Ashtara, in Southern France, near Rennes-les Bains, June 2024, on the "Throne of Isis." Also known as the "Chair of Isis," it is thought to radiate a subtle, aligning energy and be connected to Mary, a Magdalen and the Egyptian goddess Isis.

PREFACE

Ashtara

A Return to the Stars: My Home is my second book in a third trilogy and represents a significant contribution to my body of work.

My first trilogy consists of three astrology workbooks titled Your Recipe for Empowerment through Spiritual Astrology. These workbooks serve as self-help and self-learning tools encouraging students to explore their conditioned minds by self-questioning, learning astrology through the process. Each book contains exercises, stories, and challenges designed to nourish and expand the mind.

My second trilogy of books, called Arcturus Astrology, is a deep exploration of my cosmic experiences in various star systems, as well as the advanced astrological teachings I received from the Arcturians at their "round table." I feel incredibly fortunate and honoured to be the recipient of their teachings.

With this latest and third trilogy, I began with A Story Never Ever Told: A Reveal. It is a revelation! The telling exposes humanity's original path, which was distorted thousands of years ago and how the correction has occurred: a spiritual awakening and a shift in consciousness.

I feel honoured to share this next instalment of my soul's journey with you in this book, A Return to the Stars: My Home. It is the story of my travels from the Light of the Stars to the density of planet Earth and the process of my return home.

The Arcturians, Mary, a Magdalen, with Djwhal Khul (D.K.), sometimes known in esoteric circles as The Tibetan, provide their perspectives on this unfolding narrative.

Founded on guidance from Mary, a Magdalen, it seems I am to leave a legacy, the College of Cosmic Consciousness. It is intended to serve as a guide for students on their path of soul remembrance and a way to accelerate the raising of human consciousness.

A Return to the Stars: My Home is a second cosmic key for the Age of Light, that sets the stage for book three.

As with all of my words, you are invited to read slowly, reflect deeply, and feel the resonance of my words. Let your heart, not only your mind, be your guide. I share my truth. It is for you to ascertain whether it is yours.

***

INTRODUCTION

Ashtara

Welcome and thank you for choosing to read this book. Much will be revealed that may surprise and astound.

The desire to develop spiritually so I could be of service to the Divine Plan for the evolution of the human soul has been my motivation for most of my adult life. Faith and trust in a divine order based on unconditional love have been the key to attaining my goal. It's an ongoing journey. I reflect on my life and wonder how all the seeming miracles occurred so easily and simply. I learned to flow with the rhythms of life.

Prior to incarnation and upon agreement with my soul group, I chose to again enter into the 3D earth plane, this time between the two World Wars. I chose Australia because of soul memories of lives lived previously in this most ancient of lands. Barbara, my birth identity, was born on 6th July 1937. She birthed as an experiment in order to demonstrate how three different aspects of the one soul could, at different times, inhabit the one body in one lifetime.

Should the experiment work, many other souls could safely choose to do the same. Rather than the long process from birth to adulthood, a more convenient process for accelerated soul growth would be available. I am an experiment and a way-shower.

As with most humans entering the world of form, amnesia, the forgetfulness of soul purpose, engulfed my mind following the long and difficult birth.

Learning to read at an early age led me to devour religious and mystery books. My father used to ask why I would sit in the cold lounge room to read the bible when other areas of the house were heated. I needed privacy, peace and space. I searched for truth, a truth that resonated in my heart. I knew there was something in the bible that had meaning, but I couldn't find it. What I read didn't feel right. I persisted with Christian religious teachings until I married, left Australia and went to live in Fiji, where two of my children were born. My husband and I lived in a remote mining area where I conducted my own Easter and Christmas religious ceremonies.

Upon returning to Australia five years later, I yearned to experience church life again. The rose coloured glasses of my religious ideal shattered into a thousand pieces when a minister of the church attempted to sexually molest me. A dark and cold shadow enveloped my heart, remaining for twenty-nine years—a Saturn cycle.

Astrology found me. Meaning and a spiritual purpose for living life again arose within me. This pathway to know myself offered many opportunities. Self-realisation came through learning. By applying the teachings to myself, I could assist others in finding their way to do the same. Through devoted daily meditation, I became a cosmic scribe, developing inherent natural gifts. I was aware of loving and supportive celestial and extra-terrestrial guides and allowed them to train me to develop extra-sensory perception. One aspect of this broad training was telepathy, and this led me to scribe the transmissions I heard in my mind into my first five small books.

My life was full. I loved teaching astrology. I incorporated spirituality and metaphysics into my programmes. I saw these three subjects as a path to higher consciousness. I applied them to my life and taught my students to do the same. In my mind, this learning journey of soul remembrance was the main purpose of incarnation.

In 1995, I was telepathically asked by my higher guidance to adopt 'Ashtara' as my legal name. One name only because it carried a particular vibration needed for the spiritual work I was to do.

I chose not to do so because of fear of what my family would say. I was happy to imagine myself being referred to as Ashtara by my spiritual guides, but I didn't have the courage to formally change my birth name. On 4th January 2000, while attending a healer's retreat, I slipped on wet concrete and broke my wrist. A huge, valuable life lesson was learned about arrogance. I had never before experienced such overwhelming shame. No longer able to write, I knew it was the experience I needed to transform my old patterning.

I needed to drive my spiritual growth forward by following my inner guidance, rather than denying it. With immense fear, I applied to the Births, Deaths and Marriages governmental department for a legal change of name form. With shaking hands, I signed the change of name document with my non-dominant hand.

In early October 2000, I experienced a blissful ascension process described in my book, I Am an Experiment - An Extraordinary Spiritual Adventure. I observed the soul aspect of Barbara gracefully ascend through my crown chakra into the light column above it while simultaneously, a different soul aspect, Ashtara, descended through the same light column and entered into my body through my crown chakra. The experiment began.

For many months, I floundered in a world I knew not. Like a drugged zombie, I was unable to function effectively in the 3D world of form. I quickly learned to watch people around me do everyday things so I could copy them. When I reflect on the weeks, months and years following the experiential ascension, I'm amazed at how I managed day-to-day activities.

Fortunately, I had written the date and time of my ascension in a journal, so I was able to construct a new birth chart for the Ashtara personality that now inhabited my body. Expansive travel and huge spiritual growth occurred throughout the life of this new personality.

The world opened its arms to embrace me as I followed, and continue to follow, the feelings of love and joy in my heart.

The birthing process of my third personality in early January 2022 was completely different and the unusual process is described in the following first chapter. During it, I was given the name of Rose. Ashtara Rose. No way was I going to go through the legalities of another name change! I decided I would use the name Rose when filling out non-legal forms.

I later discovered that the name Rose is a title that comes from an ancient spiritual sisterhood dedicated to preserving the feminine sacred wisdom teachings. This made sense because, many years ago, a clairvoyant had seen a tree of roses in my body and had wondered what it meant. At that time, I was also perplexed, but now it makes sense. I've been sharing sacred wisdom teachings for three decades from a feminine perspective and have clear memories of being trained as a priestess of Isis in the Egyptian mystery Schools, and of having set up a Mystery School high in the Andean Mountains at Machu Picchu in Peru.

I learned that members of the gnostic teachings of The Sacred Rose were and are sacred wisdom keepers. Their soul wisdom has been gathered and practiced over many incarnations and is based on divine feminine energy. This divine feminine archetypal energy has manifested in many forms over the astrological Ages. In this incarnation I have experienced being a manifestation of The Rainbow Serpent, the divine Mother of the Aboriginal people of Australia; Lady Meru, the divine Mother of the Andean Mountains people of Peru and Bolivia; Isis of Egypt; Tara, the feminine Buddha of Tibet and Mary, a Magdalen of Israel.

Each of these archetypes represents the Divine Mother Goddess, the Feminine Ray of Energy. This Feminine Ray enters our planet at Lake Titicaca, located on the border between Peru and Bolivia.

The Mother Goddess holds the key to eternal wisdom and is the original creator. She is the void into which a seed of consciousness is planted. She symbolises the qualities of love, compassion, receptivity, allowance, truth and the wisdom gained from much experience over many incarnations. She contains within her memory banks the wisdom and knowledge of the stars.

As I currently understand, there were originally twelve groups or tribes of women who formed the basis of the Sacred Rose wisdom teachings. The Divine Feminine Goddess led each group of women. The rose is the flower symbol of this sisterhood operating under the influence of Venus, the Goddess of Love. I first entered incarnation into this solar system through Venus. I have vivid and decidedly unpleasant memories of a fall from grace on that planet. I was very naughty! The astrological symbol for Venus was changed to that of an Ankh in the ancient Mystery Schools of Egypt, where Isis was the mother goddess archetype. Or maybe it was the opposite way around?

Yeshua knew that Mary, a Magdalen, was one who carried the ancient sacred feminine wisdom. He arranged his disciples into alternate groups of twelve men and twelve women—144 in number—to assist his work of planting seeds of love-based higher consciousness into the earth plane. Each group of the original twelve women was loosely organised into the four cardinal directions of North, South, East and West. Their work involved balancing these four earth quadrants under the guidance of the appropriate goddess and with the assistance of the angelic realms and our star brothers and sisters. The Sacred Rose sisterhood understood the system of cosmic energy that nourished the earth and was able to work with it as guided. The Arcturians, my over-arching guides, trained me to re-experience this cosmic system written about in my Arcturus Astrology trilogy of books.

In our recent history (2000 years), some of the members of the Sacred Rose Sisterhood were also Essenes, a non-religious gnostic group dedicated to advancing the consciousness of humanity. I believe Mary, a Magdalen, was one. Dr. Chris. Henderson has more to say in her website article The Legend of the Sisterhood of the Rose.

What I share with you in this book needs to be discerned through your heart and your soul's knowing. Allow your intuition to guide and your rational mind to support your knowing. Question what I bring. Weigh it up within you and should you feel a heart resonance, adopt it as a current understanding. My intent is to expand your consciousness through wisdom, care and heartfelt loving vibrations. Please pay attention to your personal awakening, that of your connection to divinity through the Christ /Magdalen Light within.

To harmonise our internal masculine and feminine, we need to bring Spirit into every aspect of our lives.

Mary, a Magdalen, provided a personal message:

> Our love for each other is felt as a harmonising vibration of warmth that begins in the heart and moves to other parts of the body. You can feel this vibration now moving to your legs as it's on the way to moving to your feet. Then it moves into Mother Earth - harmonising Spirit and Earth.

When millions of people develop this vibration, the Earth feels it. Anastasia in the Siberian taiga and our close Essene family maintained this vibration throughout our lives on Earth. It is a felt experience - a connection between the heart and the mind. Harmony and peace are the result. Allowing yourself to experience the beauty of nature without thought provides the same experience. And, who designed Nature? What brilliant intelligence? Prime Creator - the masculine counterpart to the Mother Goddess who birthed our souls into existence.

I ask you to write this in your books and teach your classes accordingly.

I am a conduit and scribe for spirit and have been for more than three decades. Able to grasp the invisible, I live my life accordingly. My invisible guidance provides me with the meaning I need to make sense of my reality. I sense, feel, hear, and experience the intricate web of existence emanating from the universal source, and I perceive the voices, impulses and revelations of cosmic forces. I use this source to guide, sustain and nourish me every day of my life. This source individualises itself as a number of spiritual guides. For the writing of this book, they revealed themselves as Mary, a Magdalen, the Arcturians and Ascended Master Djwhal Khul, sometimes known as The Tibetan. Ever-present, I allow them to guide my life because I feel their love, respect, and care for me; our precious planet and humanity upon her.

In the early years of 1990, when I experienced my first conscious awareness of these cosmic forces, my family were concerned for my state of mind and suggested medical assessments be made. I knew otherwise, even though I couldn't comprehend the changes taking place in my mind. Passionately, and with love-based intent, I vowed to do whatever I could to assist other souls struggling with so-called mental health problems. My reality was different, but so real and heart-warming, I didn't need interference from rigid societal beliefs that belied my experiences. I chose to teach others what I was learning through my experiences. The grounding method I chose was astrology. The esoteric sciences were the additional forces of light.

The development of faith and trust in my inner guidance solidified with each new step taken. Patience was learned, along with detachment from other people's opinions of me. I became a conscious scribe for cosmic sources, able to translate the transmissions given, feeling as I did so the vibration of immense love within the words. It is this vibratory feeling I trust you, the reader, will feel as you read.

Not all will resonate with my story and it may confound many. I ask you to be discerning and listen to the truth of your soul's memories as you feel them as sensations within your body. Pay attention to your inner world and allow your truth not mine reveal. Through experience, I learned we each create our own world by our thoughts. Changing our thoughts about a situation creates the experience. My life is my own creation and I willingly take responsibility for it. I ask you to do the same for yours. Should you believe that your life is unbounded, it will be so. Become your own teacher and find your own source of knowledge within. May you allow the Light of your Truth illuminate your way forward.

SERPENTS OF WISDOM

Ashtara

Ever since I can remember, I have seen small, clear images of serpents floating or drifting in space in front of my eyes. These snakes or serpents are about three inches long and a quarter of an inch thick. They are visible in an outlined form rather than as solid matter. They move through space as if animated by an internal force. I only see them when it is a bright, clear, sunny day, the sky is blue, and my mind is relaxed. I could be walking along a beach or lying on my bed with the bright sunlight coming through the window. I've often played games with these images, but mostly I watch them, often wondering about their meaning and function. I have never spoken of them to another person. There didn't seem to be any need to do so. Maybe others also see them?

I feel I'm on the brink of understanding their relevance and why they are in my life.

According to well-known esotericist Helena P. Blavatsky, in her book Isis Unveiled, "the supreme, first principle, produced an egg; by brooding over [it], and permeating the substance of it with its own vivifying essence." The active creative principle, the law of evolution, then took over and set in "motion the potencies latent in it", forming suns and stars. The immutable law of harmony was set in motion and peopled with every form and quality of life." From the water came slime, and from this mud, emerged the snake—matter (p.146).

The ancient Egyptians created a simple symbol for this creation: a serpent in a circle, head joining tail, known as an Ouroboros. Spirit is symbolised by a circle and matter by the snake. This simple symbol demonstrated the union between Spirit and matter, which is the spiritual evolution of our species. It is this evolutionary process that is accelerating on Earth now.

I am a curious individual. I continually ask questions of my soul (my Higher Self). The new question became: "Is what I regularly see, when the sky is blue and my eyes are open, the first step in the evolution of matter?"

And yet another: "What about the shedding of the snake's skin?"

In metaphysical understanding, this process of a snake shedding its skin represents the psychological transformation from one state of being human to another. It can be regarded as psychological alchemy. Is there more?

The reptile sheds its skin as it grows too large for the old one. So too, do we humans cast off our "old skins" as we evolve into the embodiment of greater light, renewing our existence with greater vitality and inner strength of conviction in a higher power. Our psychic abilities increase and wisdom begins to enliven our minds. We choose to never, ever play the dark game of life again, focusing only on the Light. This decision is a choice we can all make.

Ashtara
August, 2025

***

Part One: Ascension

ASCENSION

Narrated by Mary, a Magdalen, the first part of this story details Ashtara's profound initiation experience at Lake Titicaca where she underwent a sarcophagus initiation similar to those in Atlantis and the Great Pyramid of Egypt. This process led to even greater self-realisations followed by the embodiment of Mary, a Magdalen within her womb.

***

Mary, a Magdalen, says:

From the high altitude of the Andean mountains surrounding Lake Titicaca, where an earlier Mystery School existed extending underground for long distances, you [Ashtara] agreed to be placed in a sarcophagus as a final initiation into your soul's history. This was the path of all initiates into the Great Mysteries. You also remembered a similar experience in Atlantis and the Great Pyramid of Egypt.

Immediately following the closing of the sarcophagus lid darkness engulfs and dark unconscious emotions arise in the mind as archetypal images. A story emerges from them. The soul remembers. This is what happened to you when living in a cabin on your own on the outskirts of Copacabana, Bolivia. You were there to write a book, undisturbed from external influences. Disturbance through immersion into internal influences took place as you remembered. Re-living and re-experiencing these influences enabled two things. Either you would realise and take responsibility for, and forgive the perpetrators of your approaching demise, or not.

This is the Great Initiation.

You eventually realised the thought that had attracted the dark situation, took responsibility for it and forgave. Three days and three nights did you suffer, your life force weakening. Through responsible thought and action, on the early morning of the fourth day, help arrived at your door. On the fifth day, you were provided with all you needed to leave the country, your lungs weakened from the experience.

Continuing to live that life in its different guises, you stumbled. Each time you accepted responsibility for your dark thoughts, advances in your soul's evolution into greater light took place. So the initiation experience continued until the light of self-realisation overcame the darkness of ignorance.

I entered your body to speed up the process so your soul's purpose for incarnation on planet Earth over countless lifetimes could complete.

Recently, in a seeming dream, you were supported out of the sarcophagus by your invisible team, free from all former ignorance.

You succeeded in your soul's incarnation purpose as you have been frequently reminded by different members of your invisible team, who said: "Not many can do as you have. We congratulate you."

And now, to your telling of my entrance into your body to assist further remembrance.

***

SECOND ASCENSION

In this section Ashtara describes the extraordinary process of Mary, a Magdalen, entering her body as part of an "experiment," detailing her telepathic directives, a predicted planetary frequency shift, and her conscious experience of Ashtara's light body ascending while Mary, a Magdalen's light-infused baby body descended into her, a pivotal event connected to the "Shift of the Ages."

***

04/01/2022

Ashtara

Shift coming - shift coming: Food and water. Food and water, food and water.

These telepathic words came into my mind as clear and imperative directives. I am used to being a telepathic scribe for celestial and extra-terrestrial light beings and have received directives before, but nothing like this. What was going on? Because I wasn't clear, I didn't act upon the words and chose to go outside into my garden instead.

Pulling some weeds from my garden, I again heard the same words only more strongly delivered, appearing to come from the nearby tree. This time, I chose to act upon the message. Preparing a few meals, I also filled many large containers with water. My household water was stored in underground concrete tanks, and I had visions of them being shattered by forceful earth movements.

The following paragraphs describe an extraordinary experience.

The words are taken from journal entries.

05/01/2022

Early this morning, I received a message from my overarching spiritual guides, the Arcturians:

> A frequency shift, one given by Mother Earth is soon to take place. She will shake like a dog in some places….stay inside for three days and three nights with your gate shut. You will notice a change… The atmosphere will then be lighter.

Later, while eating breakfast, I again received the same message as above with the additional instructions to close all doors and windows. My inner guidance has never let me down so I prepared as requested.

Computer and phone problems arose, as well as an electronic problem with my stove. I called an electrician and he replaced the power switches. What kind of energy had created these three problems?

Needing to go to bed very early that night, I felt myself drifting into sleep when an old 'separation from love' issue with a family member arose in my mind. I did a deep forgiveness healing process and then slept soundly for seven and a half hours. I hadn't slept as soundly for years!

06/01/2022

At 4.30 am, I woke to the excessively loud sounds of rain-filled wind gusts that seemed to be building up into roaring waves. It was still dark. Guided to lie on my back to practice a yoga nidra meditation, I focused, relaxing all body parts one by one. I no longer heard the outside sounds as I concentrated on my meditation. When complete and relaxed, I decided to get up. I didn't get very far! My head felt heavy as if it was swelling under extreme pressure. The sounds outside increased in intensity. The rain was torrential. I wasn't able to function coherently. I returned to bed and slept for a further thirteen hours!

Late in the afternoon, I awakened. The sky was still dark, a dull grey. The rain continued. The wind gusts didn't appear to be as strong. I was able to eat, but then had to return to bed. I drank a lot of water. I again slept. I didn't record for how long, but it would have been for another similar amount of time.

07/01/2022

Day Two

On awakening at 4.45 am, my head was still feeling pressure, but not as much as that of yesterday. I wanted to go for my normal early-morning walk, but knew it wasn't advisable. Something else was happening; a process that was still to be revealed. The sounds of the rain and wind gusts again increased.

Maybe around 5.30 am, I received a short message of solace from the Arcturians, my current teachers and trainers.

> We have come to provide solace. You are handling the ascension process well, fully aware. For many, it is a blur. Many realisations are to come. We have your best interests at heart. Many have chosen to leave the planet at this time. We respect their choice. The side-step Earth is taking is a measure to avoid a planetary pole reversal. We notice you are tired, so we will leave you now. We will come again.

Huh? Ascension process? I had already experienced an ascension in October 2000 and it was nothing like this! I described that one in my book, I Am an Experiment. It was a blissful experience. This message was a shock; a bit too much for me to handle. I again slept.

Upon awakening, I decided to practice another yoga meditation to relax my mind, body, and spirit. As I did, I observed a brilliant golden light shining above my crown. Fascinated, I watched it expand.

The sound of the heavy rain-waves increased, becoming much louder, seemingly building up into another crescendo.

I began to feel needle-like pricks around my navel, like acupuncture needles, only these 'needles' felt much larger. As I continued my relaxation focus, I psychically saw my entire energy body release through my navel and gracefully ascend through a brilliant column of Light into the high heavens. The light body of Ashtara ascended.

I, the observer, witnessed her ascension. Relaxing my body even more, I focused on harmonising my chakras by creating an imaginary horizontal infinity symbol and placing it in front of each chakra, beginning from the base chakra to that of the crown. While focusing on my third eye chakra, I witnessed a type of 'email' swooshing into it. The email contained a large paragraph of writing. The first series of words were written in black text and the rest were blue, like hyperlinks to websites or video clips. The blue links were all underlined, occupying about seven lines of text. I continued focusing on my meditation and then heard the words "It is done, Ashtara, it is done." Huh? What was?

I wrote the above notation in my journal.

Awake and alert during the changeover process, I remained in bed repeating meaningful mantras. I was aware the entire time of the activity around my navel, where I now felt strong sensations, like burning. The main sensation around my solar plexus chakra was of emptiness. A bit like hunger, but I didn't feel hungry. I felt empty. Something had vacated that space.

Witnessing an internal wheel being turned in my solar plexus chakra, I noticed it pulling in a rope. Slow to begin with, the rotations increased. My eyes followed the rope to view what was at the end. Attached to the rope and being pulled into my womb was a newborn light-infused, chubby, happy and quite beautiful baby girl. It felt too big for the available space and I felt my navel being stretched. I can still feel it as I'm sitting up in bed writing.

Noticing around my crown and third eye an intense gold colour with thin streams of magenta mixed with it, I watched the gold encompass my entire head and energy field, slowly morphing into my normal inner sight colour of clear violet. I understood the baby now in my womb was that of the Divine Feminine, incarnate as Mary, a Magdalen, now returned to the earth plane.

It appears as though the process was an experiment, and, if successful, will be used again on others. The message I received during the second stage of resting was that the downloading process was almost complete. I likened my understanding of the process to that of changing computers. There is a waiting period while the information from the old computer is downloaded into the new one. For me, the ascension and insertion process took many hours. Not at any time during this 'shift' process did I hear a bird song. Bird song is prolific where I live, so the absence of it was a most unusual occurrence.

Aware that my internal space no longer felt empty, I again slept, waking around 8.00 am. My dog, Pippin, who sleeps in her bed on my bed, also awakened. She hadn't stirred during the above process. At 9.40 am I sat up in bed to write.

10:20 am

I awakened and received the message:

Download complete. You can now go about your business, Ashtara.

Noticing the Sun attempting to shine through the clouds, I knew light was emerging within me. I felt what appeared to be a stitching-up process taking place in the space around where the baby had been inserted.

11.00 am

I sat up in bed. Pippin stirred. She needed to drink water and go outside. I arose, dressed and took her to the back door, closing it after her. When she had completed her ablutions, she returned. My legs felt weak and wobbly. We returned to the bedroom and again rested.

Sometime during the experience, I had the vision of a team of higher-dimensional light beings sitting in front of their computers, carefully assessing the humans who had committed to their inner journey of developing Christ Consciousness. These were the ones receiving the light transfusions needed to have their old psychological bodies replaced with one of a higher frequency. Also, a new, higher frequency programme needed to be inserted into their computer brains.

In Glenda Green's book, Love Without End, Jesus Speaks (p. 37), Jesus makes the comment that the mind is made up of two parts. The first part is centred on the brain, which is an instrument much like a DNA computer. The second part is an electromagnetic field permeating and surrounding the body. The experience written above involved these parts of my mind. I understand the mind is not the brain.

I was asked to share my experience because some readers will have had, or may have in the future, similar experiences. The process I experienced was related to the prophesied Shift of the Ages, from 3D consciousness to 5D consciousness. A heart filled with love of Prime Creator is the key to accessing the higher light-filled fifth dimension. As Jesus says:

> Higher consciousness…centred on the Sacred Heart… directs through intent and is empowered by love.

12.30 pm

Feeling the process was nearing completion, I felt the need for food. Discovering my phone was still out of action, I checked my computer. It appeared to be working effectively. The wind and rain gusts had lessened. Sometime in the late afternoon, I heard a birdsong for the first time during the entire three-day process.

***

A THREE-FOLD SPIRITUAL FLAME

In this section, A Three-Fold Spiritual Flame, Ashtara helps us understand how different personalities can inhabit one body at different times.

***

Recalling a message given to me on 31 March 2018, I reconnected to my first ascension experience. The message, paraphrased, said:

> Ashtara descended from the higher dimensions to merge with Barbara's soul to become one on 2/10/2000. Ashtara's challenge is to do the same.

Apparently, I did! Ashtara Rose, a light-infused baby created purposefully in the higher realms, was placed into the womb of an aging female body living on planet Earth. Symbolic or real? I witnessed and felt it as real.

As a conscious astrologer, I constructed birth charts for these three personalities, realising they are the representation of the etheric bodies, or clear living membranes, inserted over core essence (soul). All contain information relative to the levels of soul growth experienced in the lives lived.

I've lived them, in the one body, in one life. Other people take three lives and three bodies. Sometimes more. The preceding layer filters down to the new layer of growth and this filtering process creates mental fog and stomach nausea until cleared through self-understanding and acceptance of the situation. The birth charts are invaluable in that they provide the clarity of information needed to aid the integration process.

A three-fold spiritual flame was created and anchored into planet Earth via these exchange processes. Prior to incarnation, I had agreed to do this pioneering Light work. Three personalities inhabited the one body at different times during the life of that body, each with their own unique expression, based on other life experiences. This was the triple karma I incarnated to work through and wrote about in my Magdalen Codes book.

I Am an Experiment and it appears as though the experiment has been successful.

***

A LONG HIDDEN TRUTH REVEALED

In this section, Ashtara intertwines ancient Egyptian Mystery School teachings with her personal experiences, recounting receiving a symbol from Vishnu, her merger with Isis during a Sirius experience and her inner directive to relocate her earthly home.

***

In the ancient Mystery School teachings of Egypt, the equilateral fiery red triangle is a geometric image of an esoteric teaching. This teaching of the Divine Trinity is symbolised through the Divine Father—Osiris; the Divine Mother—Isis, and Horus—the Divine child. This esoteric teaching was replayed and anchored into planet Earth 2000 years ago by Yeshua, Mary, a Magdalen, a high priestess in the Egyptian Mystery School, and their child Sar'h.

A fiery red triangle was placed into my brain through my third eye by one called Vishnu when I made the decision to study astrology. I remember it well.

At that time, I had no idea of its symbolic meaning.

In one of the books of my second trilogy, Arcturus Astrology, I described how Isis asked me to merge with her light body during one of my many visitations to the star system of Sirius.

I am an old soul who has long traversed heaven and earth. I chose to reincarnate on planet Earth whenever her life is threatened. Many ancient memories of lives lived on planet Earth lie dormant in my memory until specific places activate them. I have written about these activations in many of my books. As a conscious star seed from Sirius, I work daily with Spirit. I am also a scribe for celestial and extra-terrestrial Light beings. I enjoy and value my work of assisting others in raising their levels of consciousness through developing self-awareness. My current over-arching guidance comes from the Arcturians, star beings from the bright star Arcturus.

Following a huge rise in my consciousness level, I am inwardly directed to move to a different location to live. These directives are clear and detailed. My human side resists. I had only lived in my current location for two years when the above ascension experience took place. Three weeks after it, I was given the directive to relocate to a different area. I resisted! A leeway of six months was given.

**

A NEW LIFE IN A NEW LOCATION

This section describes Ashtara's relocation to a new home and her "spiritual expedition" to the Flinders Ranges in South Australia, where she was guided to uncover a long-hidden secret about the land's energetic connection to the human body and indigenous culture, symbolised by "serpent" rock formations representing the Earth's "spine"

***

On 24th June 2022, I moved into my new home, in a small picturesque country town surrounded by rolling green hills and beautiful views. The energy is clean and relatively uncontaminated by human and electronic pollution. Dairy cows graze in their paddocks below my home, and, on the first house inspection, my friend and I discovered a powerful energy vortex at the bottom of the large garden. The timber house was dilapidated and needed love and restoration.

From there, I was to resume teaching the sacred circle dance, Paneurythmy.

This dance and its associated beautiful music originated in Bulgaria early last century, channelled through Ascended Master Beinso Duono, (Peter Deunov). Through the groups attracted to my work, we were to increase the frequency of Light at the vortex, focusing upon Earth-stabilising work. The vortex is also a portal through which extraterrestrial Light beings make themselves known. Hundreds of nature spirits and little people gather around us whenever we dance. Through the monthly dancing of Paneurythmy and the regular equinox and solstice earth harmonising ceremonies, the build-up of spiritualised love and cosmic light increased

Receiving the inner directive to travel to the Australian Flinders Ranges, 640 kilometres north of Adelaide in South Australia, to "reveal a secret long hidden", I prepared accordingly. I was to be there for the first few days of October 2023 and asked to allow truth to reveal. A girlfriend and I were to travel together, she with her 4-wheel drive vehicle and camping material. My inner guidance asked me to take only what was needed and to prepare well. Also, I was asked to take my little dog, Pippin, because she would lead me to places I needed to go.

During the next few weeks, my friend Sharmu purchased an Atlas travel book relative to the area and asked me to read it to pinpoint exactly where in these ranges I needed to be. She was also given her spiritual mission for the journey.

Using my intuition, only one image in the entire book influenced me in my heart chakra, my truth guidance mechanism. It was of a rock art painting. I became emotional as I viewed it and knew this was where my soul was calling me to go. The main centre close to this rock art was the outback wildlife sanctuary of Arkaroola in the northern Flinders Ranges.

We prepared well, totally trusting that whatever was to be revealed would be.

I have been on many of these inwardly directed global spiritual expeditions that began in 2000. This was when I was telepathically asked by my Arcturian guides to lead groups to the sacred sites of Peru and Bolivia to dance Paneurythmy. For nine consecutive years I did this sacred work in these two countries.

These missions were threefold. As I now understand, sacred geometric patterns form in the energy fields of the dancers when danced with hearts filled with love and joy. These geometries connect with like geometries in the cosmos, providing specific information to those existing in the higher frequencies of Light. "As it is above, so it is below". Dancing in groups at the ancient sacred sites enabled access to the ageless wisdom and knowledge stored in these sites, while the group's energy assisted the stabilisation and harmonisation of Mother Earth's frequency, which has been fluctuating for many years, causing concern to those in the higher dimensional realms.

Inwardly directed to travel to Israel towards the end of 2009, I was to be there on 1st January, 2010, to follow the escape route of Mary, a Magdalen. Always, these inwardly guided adventures were miraculous. All I had to do was to follow my heart-felt guidance and intuition. I seemed to know where to go and what to do. In many of these places, soul memories emerge and I become emotional until integration and clarity emerge.

On this new adventure, I knew soul memories would be activated. My job was to record and share these memories to awaken others into remembrance of their soul's wisdom.

Upon the first sighting of the Flinders Ranges, both Sharmu and I felt warm feelings flooding our hearts. Upon entering Arkaroola wildlife sanctuary, I felt a soul connection to the land and to the long row of large rocks welcoming all visitors.

The man who created the sanctuary in 1968, Reg Sprigg, a geologist, had been searching for uranium and oil in the area.

Home to the Adnyamathanha people, their dreamtime story depicts the great serpent Arkaroo slithering into the northern Flinders Ranges carving out a huge gorge. The great serpent then retreated to its lair in the nearby Gammon ranges.

Memory flashes of my rainbow serpent birthing humanity experience at the sacred site of Uluru, written about in my Magdalen Codes book, came to mind. Was this adventure to be a continuation of that story, or maybe an addition? I felt it to be an addition.

Ancient rock formations are meaningful to the indigenous inhabitants of the land who could see into higher dimensions. In these higher dimensions, light, sound and colour appear to dance and create shapes, and even sing.

I witnessed this at Arkaroola. My soul memories have often emerged into everyday consciousness when visiting certain places upon the planet where I have lived in previous lives, many long years ago.

At the Flinders Ranges in South Australia, I saw how, during the formation of the Australian continent, these certain shapes formed patterns. A series of hills formed into the shape of a human spine, mirror reversed. ("As it is above, so it is below"). According to ancient Sanskrit understanding, on each side of the human spine, located at the base chakra, are two serpents named Ida and Pingala. Ida is feminine energy and Pingala is masculine. Just as a human being awakens to the truth of their soul's origins and history, these energy serpents also make themselves known, as I experienced at Uluru.

As consciousness grows within the human experiencing their spiritual evolutionary process, the energy serpents begin to rise up the channels at the sides of the spine towards the heart centre. When divine love is experienced and integrated as truth, the intermingling of these energies takes place at the heart chakra, where they cross over. The two serpents then rise further up the spine to the throat and third eye chakras. It's a slow dance that, when sufficient inner work has been done, these serpents move together to experience ecstatic union with divinity through the crown chakra, connecting face to face in the unified field as One Divine energy force. Internal unity and Oneness has developed! Ascension occurs as a result of this energetic process.

The rock formation of the Flinders Ranges depicts a mirror image of this evolutionary process. These ranges form the backbone of the continent of Australia. Around these ranges are many oil and gas mines extracting the lifeblood of the land, causing shrinkage.

In Aboriginal ceremonies, white ochre is painted on the skin each side of the spine representing the two avenues or pathways of the serpents' expression.

In the ancient lands of the Andes in South America, once joined by a land bridge to Australia as Gondwanaland, there are ancient carvings of huge serpents circling around the base of a certain mountain, meeting at a specific place, face to face, as the Ouroboros. In the cave-temple of the Moon in the sacred valley near Cusco is another huge carved serpent circling the inside of the large cave-temple, entering the outside open entrance to share its face and neck, welcoming all who choose to enter.

In these ancient cultures, the serpent symbolised the subconscious realms of the human mind containing ancient soul knowledge and wisdom of all that has ever been, and will be. This wisdom is accessible to those who sincerely seek to know truth.

Why was this knowledge revealed to me when visiting the Flinders Ranges during the last day of September and 1st day of October 2023?

When re-reading the Atlas Reference book, I had a resonant heart-feeling with the image of an old black and white photo of a group of aboriginal people. It was as if my soul had once been a member of this tribe. Emotions arose. I then saw a photo of the Flinders Ranges from the air, realising it resembled a human spine that holds our body in place. Maybe this "spine" at the Northern Flinders Ranges held the land of Australia together? Was this the reason I was inwardly directed to travel to the Flinders Ranges to retrieve ancient knowledge of the physical and symbolic connection our planet has to the human body?

I remembered, and saw the birthing of Gondwanaland emerging from the chaos of the turbulent ocean. I observed the spine and chakra centres being formed. I saw the rainbow serpent and her masculine counterpart intertwining as they rose together to dance. Together they formed the valleys on each side of the spine, causing the sea to gush through.

On the range, on each side of the spine, I saw the two etheric serpents. Millions of years old, sea fossils are evident at this place as they are at Kakadu National Park in the Northern Territory. Australia is the most ancient of lands, formerly underwater.

A dimension beyond the third dimension revealed itself to me at this special place. I share it as I was asked to do. Our land was split asunder in the past. Is a repeat forthcoming?

During the first day at Arkaroola, an old psychological relationship wound emerged for me to resolve and clear. My friend was the trigger. I was pleased it emerged because I needed my energy field clean to receive whatever would be the memories and downloads.

There was a gorge seemingly created down the centre of the range, dividing the range into two. Arkaroola is positioned on the rise and Chambers Gorge where the rock art is depicted is positioned down in the gorge. I likened this understanding to that of a human body realising that Chambers Gorge is situated at the memory chakra, the base of the neck.

Lyndhurst, where the ochre cliffs are situated and where my friend did her earth healing work and ceremony, is relative to the third eye chakra.

The creation and initiation stories are depicted graphically in paintings and etchings on the rock cliffs at Chambers Gorge. Every image is many metres long and high. There are many of them and they tell a story. The ancient wisdom holders left records in the best way they could.

The Arcturians transmitted the following:

> In ancient times, before the continent of Australia was formed, the sea bubbled and churned as creatures of the deep emerged on the new land, also rising from the deep. A large island known as Gondwanaland to the humans who eventually settled, cared for and loved the land as their mother. This ancient tribe emerged upon the land millions of years after its formation. This land broke into islands due to subterranean activity. The indigenous people recorded this event through storytelling and artistry.
>
> Through the same submerged activity, another break-up is to occur. The indigenous people know this. They are expecting you. You are to work with the stones. That is all for now.

I believe the subterranean activity is caused by the movement of the Pacific Rim tectonic plates. Many geologists say they are likely to collide as they have done in the distant past, destroying the land structures, including its backbone and ribs.

Images flashed into my mind of planet Earth initially as a water planet and Gondwanaland emerging from the churning chaos of the ocean. The birth was long and laborious. Rivers and lakes formed an inland sea, all part of the Divine Plan of creation. Fossils of sea creatures are found in the rocks at Arkaroola in the north Flinders Ranges and Kakadu National Park in the far north of Australia.

Eventually, after millions of years, the Rainbow Serpent birthed humanity at the red rock centre, now referred to as Uluru. The most sacred of feminine goddesses slivered from her birthing place, travelling south to the Flinders Ranges.

At these ranges, she birthed her mate.

Millions of years later, the local tribe named her mate Arkaroo.

***

THE ARCTURIAN'S REQUEST

This section reveals the Arcturians' request for Ashtara to travel to Southern France to remember and share ancient sacred knowledge. It includes messages from the Arcturians to Ashtara's supporters, preparing them for upcoming global changes and their roles in the transition to a New World.

***

Early 2024 and through Mary Magdalen's request, my over-arching spiritual guides, the Arcturians, asked me to prepare to travel to the south of France to be there at the June solstice. My purpose was to remember and to share the ancient sacred knowledge stored in the rocks of that area. Mary, a Magdalen within me is an energy I feel in my heart, soul and womb. I recognise her vibration as most warm and loving feelings that arise through telepathic communication. Apparently, the information I need to make sense of my reality is known to Mary, a Magdalen and stored in specific sacred places I will be guided to discover. It is needed to awaken others to the truth of their purpose for being.

Some from the group of my supporters, formed through a request of the Arcturians to the readers of my weekly newsletter, Cosmic Currents, were invited to travel with me to assist. The Arcturians regularly transmit messages to my supporters similar to the following:

> Dear supporters of Ashtara's work. You are soon to be called upon to follow your own unique supporting role. Unclear as it may be now, it will gradually reveal itself. We will ensure it does.
>
> Your world is to change more dramatically. There will be shocks. When you hold true to your own calling, you will be safe. We do not wish to alarm - rather, we are preparing you for times to come.
>
> Each of you has a level of mastery. It is to be used for the greater good of the planet. Stay connected to the Source of all Light and all will be well. If you feel your vibration lowering, immediately correct the limiting thought. It will take practice. Ashtara has trained you well. Practice is needed.
>
> Rapid global change is to occur on all levels. Hold your own counsel and know you have a role to play in the transition from the old to the new world taking place.
>
> We honour you for your willingness to support Ashtara. We will come again.

Within this group are sensitive seers. Their visions and messages are the leads I need to investigate further.

METAPHOR, SYMBOLS AND ARCHETYPES

This section emphasises the universal nature of symbols, especially in light of misinterpretations and cultural differences in languages. Astrology serves as a prime example of archetypes, where each planet holds symbolic and archetypal significance. We are warned that excessive mining threatens the Earth's stability and "spine," potentially leading to another planetary break-up.

***

Symbols. The reason they are universal is because languages are misinterpreted. All languages have different words and the meanings of words are different in different cultures. True meaning becomes confused in translation, so symbols are important.

An example of the archetypes I've worked with are those of astrology. Each of the planets has a symbol that is also an archetype. A pictorial symbol tells a thousand words. I learned very early in my astrology training to invoke the planets during meditations. I learned so much this way because it uses the right spatial conceptual and abstract hemisphere of the brain.

The symbolic 'serpents' are energy currents located at the base of the human spine. Think of the caduceus, the international medical symbol where the two serpents intertwine at chakra points on the human spine. When aroused in humans and the Earth through inner psychological self-realisations, committed cleansing of shadow thoughts and emotions along with purity of divine love-based intent, these two energy currents begin travelling up the human spine from the base chakra. This is a gradual evolutionary process occurring now on a global scale.

Through excessive mining and nefarious activities by humans on the north Woomera rocket range, and through excessive oil, gas, and uranium mining, the Earth's stability is threatened. The Earth's spine is weakening. It is the skeletal structure needed to hold the planet together.

Rocks and crystals also hold the Earth's stability and orbit in place. This stability is threatened.

In ancient times, Earth was split asunder and civilisations died. The subterranean activity of the tectonic plates around the planet are again likely to grate against each other as they did in ancient times when our planet first emerged. The heavy mining activities around the Flinders Ranges area I witnessed have depleted the Earth's energetic balance.

> Another break-up is to occur. You, Ashtara, have unveiled the predicament through your remembrance and are to share it.

The large rocks at the entrance to Arkaroola welcomed me to the area and thanked me for coming. The Aboriginal spirit people at Chambers Gorge guided me into uncovering a long-held secret. I share it for your information.

Realising that Chambers Gorge and Lyndhurst formed one arm of a triangle, I searched for the apex point, knowing that a triangle is the most stabilising geometric pattern. I found it at Mt. Freeling on the Strzleckie track.

At this remote place on our journey home, I drew a triangle on the red earth and planted into it three quartz crystals from the Queensland East Coast of Australia, plus the contents of a phial of sand from Jervis Bay on the South East coast of NSW, in the symbolic gesture of stabilising our precious planet Earth.

***

During the recent April conjunction between Uranus and Jupiter in Taurus, greater understanding arose within me and my supporters. Resistance came to the fore for many, including myself. We learned to move through the physical pain our fearful thoughts created in our bodies.

My inner guidance also suggested I be more willing to expand my mind to embrace higher and broader perspectives and to keep on feeling into my heart for truth of each forward movement. I thought I had been doing so, but obviously wasn't stretching myself enough!

To give an example that may support you, I'll share a recent meditative archetypal experience. I imagined myself sitting in the centre of my birth chart, observing all the archetypal characters in it. These are the players in my game of life. Decades ago, I reasoned it would be beneficial to get to know them. During a relaxing meditation, I invoked Saturn, currently moving through Pisces. He came to me as a manifestation of the grandfather I never knew and asked me to sit on his lap. I did so, and he cuddled me. I felt his love. He advised that a team of ten workers had been engaged to help him move the many layers of resistance I had accumulated during the time between the last Age of Aquarius and this current one.

I observed their first step: he asked his team to cut in half the thick stuff (like layers of canvas matting) that symbolised the amount of my resistance to the next step forward in my life. It was huge!

As the thick mat was gradually sliced in half, he told his ten workers to pull the thick resistance 'mat of forgetfulness' apart and to roll it as they did so, because it covered over the ancient scientific knowledge contained underneath it. I could see and feel the strength the workers needed to do as requested. They were exhausted! The task was accomplished. The layers of mats were rolled up and disposed of. The skin underneath appeared fresh and clean, like a newborn baby. Saturn suggested I write this and similar experiences in a journal because the experience will make more sense at a later time. I did so.

Throughout this accelerated learning process, I realised that when I sit in the winter sun, I relax, and my mind becomes more open to inner guidance and valuable self-realisations.

One of the short snippets follows.

The Arcturians say:

> Each cell in the body needs light to function at full capacity. By regularly focusing the mind on transferring spiritual Light into your body's weakened parts, healing occurs. We ask you to practice this Light exercise. Resistance to moving forward is simply an absence of light in the cells. Give them light and love, and healing occurs.

Most of my inner guidance comes during the night in the form of transmissions. Now, as I prepare for the France adventure, it is also coming during a sunny day.

The Arcturians continue:

> Atlantis was created millions of years ago. It was one of an advanced race who selected Earth as their second home. The beauty of nature and the fresh, clean air provided a place of refuge for the different races who visited the blue-green planet. Their knowledge of technology surpassed the knowledge of today.
>
> Your current world is in upheaval. Many unexplained mysteries are influencing human lives. Life spans are shortening; young people seek to find meaning where none can be found. The Age of Aquarius is breaking old information, creating chaos in most established social enterprises. Daily, man-made laws are broken, and respect for authority has diminished. History repeats. Cycles repeat. Can we learn from history? It doesn't appear to be so. The masculine interpretation of history—his-story—is no longer relevant to the developing human consciousness.

What about cycles? Planetary cycles? Can light be thrown on human development through cycles of time?

A new Age of Aquarius has begun. When was the last Aquarian Age? Twenty-six thousand years ago. Twenty-four thousand BCE. An advanced civilisation known as Atlantis was thriving, more technologically advanced than our civilisation today. Atlantean people generally lived in tune with the cosmic forces and those from the land. Some historians refer to this Age as a Golden Age of Peace.

Long ago a race of beings lived long lives on your planet. Some lived for more than a thousand years. Your Bible is a testament to this. How were they able to live so long?

The answer is simple. They understood the nature of life-force energy. Now-a-days some call this energy prana or chi. Readily available for all to use, it is discouraged by the governments and those in authority who rule the people. Money cannot be made from free energy.

Many civilisations have lived on Earth. All have destroyed themselves. Your current civilisation is also in the process of so doing.

Many of the specie in other realms decided to prevent yet another disaster. Because of a universal non-interference policy, a way needed to be found to halt the destruction process. The way chosen was to awaken the human race to the fact of their knowledge from the stars and their connection to the Source of all energy. We sought to educate by providing ways and means for you to become self-realised.

A long, slow process by your timing, it is now accelerating. The energy we provide enables minds to open to broader, higher perspectives and hearts to open to the experience of divine love.

Through these shifts in perception, a major calamity is being avoided. It won't be long before the truth of human origin is realised by the masses. In your timing, this awakening to truth process has taken almost 26 thousand years, from one Age of Aquarius to another.

We will elaborate on this timing process.

***

As we gather our forces to work with you, Ashtara, we observe your energy field. It is considerably lighter than yesterday. We congratulate you on moving through lifetimes of a belief no longer needed. The extraction of the energy in which the belief resided was the healing method needed. Pain is simply a blockage of belief.

And now to continue with the theme of timing. On Earth, your timing is different to other planets and star systems. Your timing method is dependent upon the Sun. Solar timing. In parts of your world, some indigenous people use the timing of the Moon. Others use a Mayan calendar. Some others use a Hebrew calendar. So what timing method is used by the majority of the population? Solar timing.

The Sun rises and sets daily, seemingly at different times and dependant upon time zones.

What if there were two Suns in the sky? How could this influence life?

These two Suns shone on the Atlantis landscape for most of the former Age of Aquarius. How, then, could humans live there through solar timing?

Know that there is life on many planets and stars. Different life forms exist on them. Some human-like; some animal or insect life. Planet Earth is where human life began. Seeds of consciousness from other places were planted. Like plants, they need the light of the Sun to survive.

Species from other star systems and planets often visited Earth. It was their playground.

***

JOURNEY TO FRANCE

Ashtara details her mission to France with her support team, former members of the Sisterhood of the Rose, to reactivate Atlantean consciousness and resurrect Mary, a Magdalen's ancient wisdom. The journey involved powerful, energetic clearings at old church sites, the resurrection of sacred teachings, and the formation of global energetic triangles through group efforts.

***

The mission I was given in early 2024, by my regular over lighting spirit guides, the Arcturians, consisted of three parts. It concerned my support team, a group of mainly women, all former members of the ancient Order of the Sisterhood of the Rose.

First part of the Mission

Upon the request of Mary Magdalen to the Arcturians, I was asked to journey to France with the women from my volunteer support group who chose to come. My personal spiritual service work was to access a dormant part of my right brain that contained a strand of the ancient sacred wisdom teachings Mary a Magdalen knew so well. I figured this would be relative to esoteric/evolutionary astrology because it was in 1996, when I began my training in evolutionary/esoteric astrology, that Mary Magdalen first made herself known to me saying she wanted to assist me to remember and reclaim this wisdom strand from within my soul's memories.

Those of us who had been inwardly so guided, intuitively and lovingly returned the land to its pristine energetic state awakening the Atlantean consciousness that had been deliberately sealed over thousands of years ago. I was told that the southern area of the Pyrenees mountains was a physical remnant of Atlantis, and that some of the shadow activities that caused the demise of Atlantis had been captured and stored in the area around the little church we visited, as well as inside it. Horrific denigration against women had taken place here.

Fifteen women from six different countries nestled into the small town of Quillan, situated in a valley surrounded by the southern Pyrenees mountains. The river Aude ran through the village, and we understood it was along this river that Anna, Grandmother of Jesus, Joseph of Arimathea her son, Mary Magdalen and their families travelled after Jesus' crucifixion experience, seeking their new home in this foreign land. This new home was to be with a group of fellow Essenes already living in an existing settlement situated close to the base of Mt. Bugarach in the Languedoc area of southern France.

In this area, Mary Magdalen was and still is much loved and worshipped. It is where she taught her perspective of the ancient sacred mysteries she had learned in the Egyptian temples of Isis. Prior to his crucifixion Yeshua had asked Mary to teach the Way of Light she had learned from him combined with her training as a Priestess of Isis. My mission was to remember this knowledge and share it.

I was also asked to teach my group the sacred circle dance Paneurythmy, and to dance it at sunrise on the solstice, 21st June. Nature rejoiced as we danced dressed in white beside the river Aude, the water gurgling and sparkling in the early morning rays of the Sun. We danced again on the 22nd June 2024.

The group shared their unity, joy, love and light with the local community and with Nature. We gave so much joy to the bakery owner she cried when we left the area. Quillan was the perfect place to stay for the ten-day sacred mission.

My mission was accomplished through experience. When experiencing, I feel and know truth. What were they? I'll briefly share the first.

As a group, we travelled up a long, winding and narrow road in our hired van until we reached a tiny and very old, seemingly dilapidated church situated on the top of a hill. The surrounding countryside was incredibly beautiful. Entering the church, I began to feel uncomfortable. Walking towards the front righthand side of the tiny church to be close to the many framed paintings and drawings of Mary Magdalen, I stopped. Mary was uncomfortable within me, saying the energy in the church needed cleaning. My friend passed on her message to activate the cleansing. I did. Standing in front of the altar, I asked the group to tone from their hearts the sound of OM. The harmony created by the continuous sound of fifteen women was incredibly beautiful and the created vibration immediately began clearing the dense energy inside the church. Light filled the internal space where dark, energetic shadows of masculine violence against women had previously existed. More work needed to be done - outside.

I intuited there was a powerful vortex underneath the building that needed clearing and reactivating with the vibration of love, so walked outside. One by one, other group members followed. Some were emotionally disturbed by what they had been psychically shown. Much violence and abusive treatment of women had taken place in earlier times in this little building.

An energetic stranglehold surrounded the building that became obvious through the distress of the first few women to emerge after me. One was crying uncontrollably, feeling as if she was being choked by an energetic rope around her neck. Another was extremely agitated and felt the need to stride vigorously around the building. I intuited these two reactions were connected and that the striding and circling needed to take place ten times. When one circuit of the church was made the energetic 'rope' around the other woman's neck released. The ten rounds were needed before the painful choking ceased. Inside and outside the church, the energy had been cleared.

Immediately this activation work completed I witnessed the cleansed, released energy speedily travel directly to the vortex at the bottom of my garden in Maleny, Queensland, Australia. From there it travelled to the vortex at Uluru, a huge, red rock monolith sacred to the

Aboriginal people of Australia. A fiery triangle formed, connecting these three earth vortices. More triangles formed around the globe. The energy moved too quickly for me to observe the other locations.

A tremendous group effort had taken place through a group of loving and aware women aligned as one with a spiritual mission based on meaning and purpose.

Two days later, at the top of the sacred mountain, Mt Bugarach where we also danced, I connected another sacred global triangle; the three mountain-top areas on our planet where esoteric training schools had been situated in earlier times. Part of the wisdom teaching is shared when dancing the sacred circle dance, Paneurythmy and all it symbolises. I learned this dance in the Rila Mountains of Bulgaria where it originated through the spiritual work of Ascended Master Peter Duenov. I was taught how the movement of the dancers geometrically connects heaven to earth at the same time as it opens the dancers' hearts to feelings of love and harmony. Throughout the practice remembrance of ancient soul memories can arise and the loving energy formed by the group creates a frequency wave that travels to wherever it is directed.

The mountains I was asked to travel to and teach this dance were the Andes, specifically at Machu Picchu in Peru; the Island of the Moon in Lake Titicaca, and Mt Bugarach in the Pyrenees Mountains of France, where I believe the Languedoc Essenes danced at Full Moons, equinoxes and solstices. This too was an esoteric training school for spiritual initiates.

When visiting a cave, situated approximately 20—25 minutes walk from Renne le Chateau, Mary, a Magdalen, told me it was in this cave she had spent many long nights often by herself but also with initiates. This was where she took them for training into higher levels of consciousness.

As she was taught in the ancient Egyptian esoteric Mystery Schools, so too did she train her initiates to undergo challenging tests to their mental, emotional, and physical states of being thus enabling greater self-awareness. Through developing an understanding of The Way of Light, initiates realised how their thoughts created their reality and how their emotional and physical states of being resulted from these thoughts.

When I had integrated this information, she asked me to stand outside the cave to survey the land and report on what I saw. Having been trained in Peru to read the topology of the land I was able to clearly see how this cave could be considered a feminine sacred site. Situated in an oval shaped grouping of hills the internal shape of the cave was like a womb, Placed high on a ridge the area below was filled with small shrubs through which a flowing creek made its way to a nearby village. This path of the creek was shaped like a uterus.

The pilgrimage mission to France was successful on many levels – spiritually, emotionally, mentally, and socially. Much was learned and realised. Love, joy, gratitude, faith and trust were the overarching binding forces.

***

MULTI-DIMENSIONAL VIEWING

Following her return from France, Ashtara describes experiencing a vivid multi-dimensional light show within her mind, filled with golden-yellow light and shimmering natural creations. She perceives this as a glimpse into a higher dimension, similar to what newborn babies experience, and emphasises the importance of retaining this natural gift of perception.

***

Upon waking a few days following my return from France, I had the good fortune to carefully observe within my mind's eye a multi-dimensional light show of intense brightness, mostly containing the colour of golden yellow. What I viewed inside my head was Nature at her finest, with so much beauty and grandeur it took my breath away. In a relaxed and open-minded state, with my heart filled with gratitude and joy, I observed a series of images all merging with each other into amazing natural creations.

Clear, bright and radiating energy of life, the creations shimmered, glowed and moved, seemingly in wave formation yet still maintaining essence. Inside my mind's eye, nothing was static. All was gentle swaying movement. The most predominant shapes were of trees. The leaves on the gently swaying trees were of bright golden yellow, although almost too bright to view. The spectacular and brilliant Light show lasted for maybe an hour before I tired. Awe-inspiring, I knew I was experiencing a higher dimension than that of 3D Earth. It seemed so close and real.

I felt incredibly privileged to have experienced this glimpse into a higher and finer dimension. I realised that what I experienced as a mature adult was also what newborn and young toddlers experience following their birth on planet Earth. They see such a beautiful kaleidoscope of brilliant colour, shapes and sizes, they are also mesmerised by them. Why, oh why, do we parents take this gift of seeing away from them? With parental encouragement, they do not need to lose this natural gift yet, because of parental ignorance, most do.

Understanding that the above vision was a gift from the higher realms as a result of my activities in France, I chose to reflect on this overseas experience and write about it as I had been asked to do.

***

Part Two: A Continuation

A CONTINUATION.
A Story, Never, Ever Told. A Reveal

This section, narrated primarily by Djwhal Khul (D.K.) and the Arcturians, provides details about the ancient history of human life on Earth, including the evolution of our early ancestors, the arrival of different races, and Ashtara's past lives. They introduce current life as a "dream scape" and highlight Ashtara's role as an "experiment" for accelerated soul growth, leading to the imminent "Shift of the Ages" and her return to higher realms.

***

Djwhal Khul (D.K.) speaks:

And it came to pass with the furtherance of time, your time as you know it, your ancestors lived and connected to the land. Isolated, without contact to any other specie, they survived and eventually thrived for millennia.

From the Martians, they developed a warring element to their nature.

Tribe against tribe. They wandered the vast land, even travelling across the ocean in their small canoes. No other specie did they meet.

They survived and remembered, through storytelling, dance and paintings. Some chose to live on the eastern shore where the climate was more conducive to survival. Some chose the isolated west. Different languages were developed according to the areas lived. Few remained in the centre of this vast land.

Change was slow, very slow.

From another country, way across the vast ocean, came two brothers bringing with them another culture and beliefs.

Not as primitive, and with lighter skins and different bodies, they interacted with the local inhabitants.

Interbreeding took place on the eastern shore and harmonisation between the two races occurred. Records were created, etched and painted inside cave walls. The evolution of the human soul continued.

One thing constant in life is change. Slow at first and then quickening, as if by a planned design.

Some hundreds of years passed before another specie from a far distant land discovered the vast southern hemisphere continent. These people also had lighter skin and claimed the land for themselves.

Yet another race of people arrived with a more serious and deliberate intent. They needed a far-away land to house their prisoners, those who had done unlawful but not life-threatening deeds. The land down-under was perfect. Isolated. Their sea vessels could also take adventuring souls who were keen to begin a new life in a land of plenty, or so it appeared to the specie landing on the eastern shores. These people came armed with weapons of destruction, claiming the land for their king and country. Huge changes occurred.

Free white settlers also arrived as they had been enticed by their far-away government to travel vast distances across the sea to begin a new life in a country they called Australia.

After serving their prison sentences, released prisoners received small parcels of land on which to settle and begin a new life. The white skinned men took for themselves the dark skinned women. A mixed race was born. The Martian influence multiplied.

Many times did you return to this land, Ashtara, to harmonise karma, mostly experiencing lives in the Australian centre. Now clear of the Law of Cause and Effect, it's time to leave the earth plane to resume life in the higher realms of Light.

Briefly has your soul's history been told. Yes, you did experience some lives in a northern land and it is these lives we are to focus upon in the story to follow.

***

Ashtara speaks:

Continuing to live out the life I foresaw, my indomitable will took me to many countries my soul had previously lived. I knew the sacred mysteries. My soul remembered them. Many times, in many lives have I experienced these memories.

Another voice from within me speaks, the Arcturians:

> Your current life is a dream scape, created by your thoughts and imagination. From the time in the sarcophagus in 2011 to now, you have been remembering and reclaiming the knowledge gained through living lives as an Initiate. Entombed, sometimes for centuries because of misdeeds; at other times for the required time of three days and three nights. This is the time it takes for the soul to experience crucifixion on the Cross of Matter, the 3D plane of planet Earth, and its resurrection into the greater Light of existence without form. The opportunity is given to choose to assist the collective soul's evolution of consciousness. You chose this path.

> As did author Elizabeth Haich's experience in her memory of Initiation in the ancient Mystery Schools of Egypt, you too foresaw your future in the Age of Aquarius. As a Water Bearer, this foreseeing is imminent. Temporarily harmonised by invisible agents of Prime Creator, as per her request for help, Gaia, the Spirit of Planet Earth, prepares for the great Shift of the Ages. Debased by multitudes unwilling to see and be the Light, all souls have chosen to either evolve or experience many thousands of years of future darkness. It Is As It Is.

You, Ashtara, have chosen and demonstrated publicly amongst much opposition, your path to the Light. We, who will return to Earth to greet you once again, eagerly await our reconnection. As Elizabeth Haich foresaw, so have you. You know we speak truth and you have learned to trust us. Vast has been your storytelling of lives lived and experienced in many lands. You have recorded them well.

Who will read? This is not your concern. Two more books are you to publish this year. Yes, another trilogy. All your books act as memory triggers for readers. Your verbal teaching does the same. Those souls eager to awaken to the Light levels available on Earth will find them of great value. Your team on the inner planes has manifested as your team on the outer material realm. A long-lasting legacy do you leave for those seeking the Light. There will be much celebration on your public return to the Light realms.

And now, to the work ahead. We, the Arcturians, leave you now and will come again in like manner.

***

In like manner? A narrative you hear in your mind! Who is telling the story? Is it another part of your soul? Remember, it is your soul who has the memories of lives lived in other lands, including that of the narrater. We, like you, are scribes. We tell a story. You dear Ashtara, simply write what you hear. A simple request. We thank you.

***

THE BAR

Continuing D.K.'s narrative, this section marks the beginning of Ashtara's new phase of life (starting January 7, 2022), detailing significant personal changes, including relocation and adapting to Mary, a Magdalenas embodiment within her. It touches on Ashtara's efforts to recover long-lost memories of human origins through travel to lands of her past lives, such as India and Tibet, and her commitment to Mary, a Magdalen, to create a College of Cosmic Consciousness as her humanitarian legacy.

***

D.K. speaks:

>Now, out of the sarcophagus, you will notice subtle changes. Initiation at that level is accomplished. Yes, fourteen years, a Saturn cycle.

>Beginning a new book can be daunting or exciting. What do you choose?

Ashtara: Exciting!

D.K. continues:

>And, so it is.

From the time when you chose to be placed in the sarcophagus until now, much has been experienced. The new life began on 7th January 2022, as recorded. From then to now you struggled to make sense of the new reality. Following still your inner guidance, you left a life in an area well known since 1976 to begin life in a new town further north. New friends were made, old habits and ways of life were left behind. Family was left behind. Neptune and Pluto contributed much to your new life. A consciousness-raising process and an acceleration experienced.

Remembering, remembering, existing multi-dimensionally, you began to consciously create a new life. Sensitive to an extreme, guarding your energy levels took observational focus and attention to detail. Unable to spend much time in the lower vibrational levels, you instigated many necessary changes to your everyday life.

Mary, a Magdalen, now embodied within you, became a greater influence.

At first, it was strange to have another soul occupying your body, and many adjustments were needed. Daily afternoon rest times were required to maintain equilibrium and the sequential emotional strength to conduct your new classes. Eager students wanted more of you and you gave your loving energy freely.

Recovering memories from the beginning of human life on planet Earth was part of your new life, as was storytelling and dance. To recover these memories required travelling to other countries where your soul once lived. These recovered memories follow.

**

D.K. continues:

Lives lived in the Northern Hemisphere.

Ashtara: Where?

D.K. :

India, the East.

Trained by Sai Baba, a devotee, you lived in the south of India.

And it came to pass that in a life lived in India, you, the soul aspect of Ashtara, lived a life of spiritual training by one known as Shiri Sathya Baba. A male in this life, you lived in relative solitude, devoted to your studies and spiritual life. Before this life was the one lived in Tibet as the 13th Dalai Lama. It was in the following life when you, as an astrologer to the Dalai Lama, through arrogance, fell from grace into public disgrace.

Attaining the higher levels of consciousness in former lives, but unable to maintain it, in each life the same pattern emerged.

It takes dedication, commitment and daily administration to maintain a high level of consciousness no matter the country or the time.

During this life you returned to many countries where you lived in other times, none having the memory potency as the lives lived in South America or Australia.

A long, long journey has it been and the end is nigh. You feel it coming and wonder how it is to eventuate. Healthy in body and limb, you cannot foresee a normal death any time soon, and you are correct.

Other plans are afoot. We will elaborate.

Within the illumined mind, awareness increases as the new method of communication (telepathy) takes place. The two involved struggle to comprehend. How can the two minds meet? Can the frequencies be adjusted to allow the connection? Both transmitter and receiver are anxious to connect. Not Yet!

Awakening the consciousness to a finer frequency takes time and concentration by the recipient. Intention carries weight. The transmitter's voice can seem faint. Impressions are given, sometimes received and sometimes not. It is a process of awakening. The recipient feels the love vibration from the transmitter and seeks more of it.

Through awareness, it will happen.

Slow on the uptake at first, you developed finesse, realising the narrative involved your life as a soul. Many people write memories of their life. You write memories of many lives lived by the soul in different bodies.

We have left out the lives lived in darkness, a puppet to them. You remembered these when doing your clearing and healing journey through many dark nights of the soul on the lowest level of human degradation. You experienced the horror of abusive power games as a woman; simply an adjustment of karma where, as a male, you had perpetuated the dark shadows of sexual abuse. Major life lessons needed to be learned and you did learn, suffering much throughout the many experiences.

Much have you experienced. Much have you remembered. Much have you learned. No longer will you indulge in the temptations that lead to character weaknesses.

You have learned well.

A return to the stars is imminent, but not for a few years. There is some unfinished business to attend to first. Humanitarian work for the greater good of the collective whole is at hand. Educational work. A College is to be created, with the focus on consciousness.

A Consciousness College lived. Your teachers are those trained in other lives in cosmic consciousness. You are the headmistress, a role you have played in many other incarnations.

The next part of our narrative explains some of the subjects.

From the darkness of ignorance you have lived in countless lives to the brilliant Light of higher consciousness. Your journey has been long. Your story is inspirational, following your aspiration to know yourself and to uncover and be your potential. You have risen through layers and layers of dense psychology.

Following the Light of Spirit has been your commitment and now the culmination of your life's work as an educator is at hand.

We congratulate you.

Much have you already shared in your books, articles and teaching. More are you to share through your legacy.

We salute you.

We will come again with more details.

***

A NEW CREATION

In the following section, Mary, a Magdalen, outlines her perspective on the development of the College of Cosmic Consciousness. She indicates that the college will initially operate online, with its subjects provided by the Arcturians and Merlin, and guided by an invisible team, allowing students to progress at their own pace towards a more profound understanding of the "Great Mysteries".

***

Mary, a Magdalen, shares her perspective:

And so, Ashtara Rose, our story is being told. Who will read it? That is not our concern. We have a College of Cosmic Consciousness to create and establish. Many happy hours will be spent doing so. Who will attend? Will it be physical or online?

We will begin online with a website. You have the domain name.

The Arcturians and Merlin have given you the subjects.

Your invisible team will assist the creation and the teaching and will work with each student according to their allowance. Each student of the Great Mysteries will work at their own pace. When each new level has been reached, the bar will rise higher, as the next level becomes available to them.

As it is in life, so it will be in the higher realm. I suggest you write of this development in detail so your readers are informed. I will add more when the time is right.

***

THE COLLEGE OF COSMIC CONSCIOUSNESS

The following is a detailed curriculum created under galactic guidance to be developed by Ashtara and her Mission Camelot team.

TOPICS TO AWAKEN CONSCIOUSNESS

Level One: Introduction to the Inner Life of the Soul.

1. Cosmic Astrology
2. Numerology
3. Tarot—The Science of Images, according to Mary, a Magdalen
4. Dream Interpretation
5. Meditation—enabling concentration and focus.

***

Level Two: Mind Expansion & Mental Agility.

1. Cosmic Astrology.
2. Esoteric Healing - as wave forms.
3. Science of Triangles- as cosmic language forms.
4. Tarot - the Science of Images.
5. Introduction to The Seven Rays of Creation.

***

Level Three: Opening the 3rd Eye to Inner Sight.

1. Cosmic Astrology.
2. Right Use of Will and Power.
3. Psychic Sensitivity.
4. Meeting and working with your Inner Teacher.

***

Level Four: Remote Viewing & Intentional Multidimensional Travel

1. Cosmic Astrology in action. Preparing the teachers.
2. Conscious unification/harmonisation between mind and heart.
3. Connecting to your star home and family.
4. Identifying your Soul's purpose of incarnation and consciously choosing to work with it in service to the Divine Plan (the evolution of the human soul).

***

Level Five: Galactic Consciousness.

> These students (Level Five) are the Initiates who have worked on themselves through all the levels and are now preparing for their final initiation, the major work in the land of form, planet Earth. The five Ashtara's are to arrange the content. Your galactic team will guide and provide the details.

***

The above is according to the guidance of Merlin as a transmitter for the Arcturians and Mary, a Magdalen.

***

Introducing Sammie, in another life the first daughter of Mary, a Magdalen born following Yeshua's crucifixion. Ashtara recognised her familiar soul energy while viewing a video about autists. Mary, a Magdalen created the telepathic connection between Sammie and herself in the etheric realms. She is a wise old soul.

Mary's message to Ashtara:

> Sammie has agreed to transmitting her educational messages with me, and naturally with you. These will not be shared elsewhere. She has been waiting for this moment in your time to begin. You are to keep records and type them. It will form the curriculum for your Cosmic Astrology course; expanding upon the Arcturian's training. They are in agreement.
>
> Monumental in content and design, they, like nothing else available in your third-dimensional world, will accelerate the raising of human consciousness; our dream and aspiration is about to manifest.

3/06/2025

Merlin says:

> ...Camelot and the College of Cosmic Consciousness:
>
> Good name: You now have the subjects, the structure and now all you need are the teachers. You already have seven. This is enough.

Sammie will advise the autist's requirements. There is to be a special area for their teaching/sharing, and also for the healthy children. You have this group of teachers (the 'mothers').

Planning: Jan has her team and may need more.

Healers: Sammie will guide.

It will all fall into place according to your allowance.

***

03/06/25

Mary, a Magdalen's guidance.

> ....and now to Sammie. She has communicated with her mother about you and I so all can proceed with correct protocol. There is another in the Camelot group whom Sammie is to communicate with on a different topic, or subject as you call it. Our communication is to focus on Cosmic Astrology. Sammie is excited, as am I.
>
> It will stretch your mind, Ashtara.

04/06/25

Good morning, Ashtara.

> Merlin's message and mine connect.

The special area of the website for Sammie and my teaching is to be called:

Adventuring into the Cosmos Astrology: Cosmic Astrology.

Teaching given by Sammie, Mary, a Magdalen and Ashtara Rose.

We begin,

Why have you fallen from Grace into ignorance of your inheritance from the stars?

Why did you choose, as a specie, to forget your origin and descend into the glue of matter?

Captured for aeons of time by the dark of your own mind, the time of return to the Light is imminent.

Step by step, you will be guided on your path of soul remembrance.

How far, and at what pace, you travel is entirely up to you.

Our aim and aspiration as your teachers is to do what we can to raise your level of conscious self-awareness that enables revelation of the light of truth.

Will you join us?

***

And then comes the Initiation into the Great Mysteries teaching, combined with those of The Way.

Archetypes, images, and sacred geometry, in particular, triangles and pyramids.

Now you have the content outline for the College subjects.

Encouraging harmonisation of the right and left hemisphere of the brain is indeed important.

***

A LONG LIFE LIVED

In the following continuation of Ashtara's extensive soul journey on Earth, Djwhal Khul (D.K.) confirms it is reaching its conclusion. Ashtara is congratulated on overcoming significant spiritual challenges, and we are told of her imminent and public "return to the stars". Her pioneering role as an "experiment" is emphasised as it has "paved the way for others."

***

Djwhal Khul (D.K.) continues his narrative:

Within the contours of time, have you lived and travelled Ashtara, and now your story of a long live lived as a soul, learning and experiencing on planet Earth, is coming to a close.

A new life beckons, faintly at first. The life of a soul is indeed long until its return and eventual merging with the Source from which it was birthed. You feel the wisps of this call and are preparing accordingly. A legacy are you preparing to leave. You have the support of your invisible team in doing so.

Our narrative has another chapter to be written and it is forthcoming.

We begin:

A long list of achievements have been accomplished on your journey through the dark nights of the soul into now Ashtara. Dispelling the dark has not been easy, yet you have persisted. Not many have done as you have. We congratulate you. And now to the final chapter of your soul's journey on Earth.

A return to the stars is imminent and preparation needs to be made accordingly.

I am Djwhal Khul, sometimes you have known me as Kuthumi. I have been calling for your return for some time. Yesterday, you were shown an image, and your focus was on the millions of stars in the sky. We felt your longing to return. This was our signal, and so the preparation begins.

As you have noticed from some of our random impressions, we are coming to Earth for you and it will be public, viewed by a small collection of people. Being a pioneer and an experiment, it is normal for you. You have enjoyed the role and it is to continue. We will provide more images when the timing is right. You will make the connections and take appropriate action accordingly.

That is all for now.

***

THE LIGHT OF DAWN

Ashtara shares a vision of a "brilliant sunrise," symbolising a new beginning, while D.K. reinforces she is prepared for her "new life in the stars." This section highlights the increasing importance of ancient zodiacal knowledge and celebrates Ashtara's achievement in reaching higher states of consciousness, acting as a "pioneer in the consciousness realms" illuminating the path for others.

***

Ashtara comments:

Dark one moment, eyes close again to rest before rising to begin my day. Opening my eyes again, I witness a brilliant sunrise, the bright light of dawn. A moment of blessedness. A new light emerges as the new day dawns, full of promise. What shall I do with it?

Enjoy it, in wonder and appreciation of the great gift of Nature, or ignore it. I choose to enjoy it.

***

D.K. says:

> You will have all you need, Ashtara, for your new life in the stars. You were born into this life on Earth with

nothing and so you will leave it. We will show you glimpses of what is to come when the time is right.

So, what are you to do with my narrative? Share it in your new book. What else?

***

And so the knowledge of the zodiac is to become more widely known as an instrument through which ancient knowledge can be understood and integrated. Some say it is God's System of energy management. No matter the name, the influence of the energies compels all humans to be a certain way. You, dear Ashtara, are learning to view the system of astrology you learned in earlier years in a different way, one more profound and advanced.

I ask you to be even more alert to my calls as I have much information to convey.

The small percentage of error needed to be navigated is important for the life of the soul on Earth. Many people on Earth have not made the grade. You, Ashtara, are one who did. By this act alone, you are noticed and much attention given to you. We have often said that not many have done as you, and now you know what we mean.

You have been captured by the lure of planet Earth for aeons of Earth years; however, in the life of a soul, it is simply seen as a hiccup. Your return to the higher realms is imminent. There will be celebration in the light realms. Your soul family of origin await your return. So many challenges have you overcome, mostly consciously, and now is the final one: your legacy. You have known you are to leave a legacy without understanding what it was to be.

From your birth's personality's ascension to the light, Ashtara's walk-in of descent from the light into your body, to her ascension to allow Mary, a Magdalen, to embody within your womb, the experiment proceeded. You have paved the way for others to follow. Long will you be remembered.

From your perspective, you had a job to do and it will be achieved. Nothing can stop it. We leave you now and will come again to conclude our narrative.

***

Entrance into the great circle of the sky requires acute self-awareness of the higher mind and observation of the wisps that arise within it. An initiation.

When harmonisation between the human and the soul occurs. It takes years of meditation practice to achieve. It is possible, as evidenced by the avatars of the earthly realms, to accomplish. Silence and focus are contributing factors. Buddha and Jesus, who became Christed, are examples. There are other humans on the planet now joining them in this state of elevated consciousness, a holy place in the mind where reverence for nature and its many gifts are necessary.

The highest level of consciousness is attainable by those who take the holy path of Light. Through daily practice, dedication and commitment, it can be attained.

The faint wisps given to the human by those in the higher realms gradually become meaningful. The inner light reveals more secrets. Where former dark images containing stories appeared, now the images are filled with light. A wonder to behold.

You, Ashtara, have moved in consciousness to this level. Light literally fills your mind. Images appear as if lit by a brilliant light. You have turned the light switch on in your mind, allowing the brightness to fill former dark spaces.

Aware of chakra activity, and connecting the two is also part of your experiences. You share your experiences as a guide to seekers of the light.

Your written words act as street lights illuminating the dark.

Not many have done as you.

A pioneer in the consciousness realms, you light the way for others to follow.

Your narrative has one final chapter to write. We ask you to prepare accordingly. I am Kuthumi, calling you home, as I said I would so long ago.

THE LIFE OF A SOUL

In this section, D.K. elaborates on the soul's long journey, including a "fall from Grace" when choices were made "from a place other than love." He stresses that love and conscious thought are essential for ascent and reconnection to the Divine Source. This section emphasises Ashtara's personal journey of self-realisation and her dedication to teaching others, concluding that she leaves a powerful legacy of love and wisdom through her books and the College of Cosmic Consciousness.

***

D.K. continues:

It began slowly, Ashtara, the creation of your soul's history, and gathered pace as karma accumulated. The life of the soul is long in Earth years, and for you, an old soul, it has been millions of years.

The fall from Grace was gradual and occurred naturally as choices were made. When a choice was made from a place other than love, karma accumulated and attracted like. It seems to be the way of all souls on the third-dimensional plane of matter. A veil descends over the mind with each fall. Thought and the intent behind it, when devoid of love, accelerate the descent. Memories accumulate and the internal waters muddy with them.

And yet, there is always the glimmer of light. Where can it be found?

Love is always the key to begin the ascent. Love and conscious attention to thoughts.

Electromagnetic fields are your bodies. The mind can become overstimulated with too much electricity and short-circuit. A separation from the Source of power takes place, akin to a disconnection from an electrical circuit. To replug into this Source of power often requires assistance. Reconnection is available at all times, yet needs to be requested. We in the higher realms wait to be asked. We will not interfere. We did once, to our detriment.

We watch over you as our children. We love you dearly and are amazed by your creations.

Your story, Ashtara, is similar to many others, although a little longer than most. Much have you learned as you travelled through time and space, mostly forgotten until now.

Through determination and choice, you began the ascent into greater light. Challenging it has been, yet you persisted. Learning to feel the vibration of Prime Creator's love within you, you wanted more. Like a soothing sedative, this love began to be remembered, and you chose to fill your heart and mind with it. Recognising the vibration, you learned to self-create it. No longer did you need to call upon another for help. You learned your capacity for love and chose to reconnect with Source daily.

Deciding to teach others to overcome their shadows through self-realisation and self-love, you did so for decades. Books were written about the steps to take along the way. Awakening others to truth and love of the Divine Creator, the Mother Goddess who births all souls into existence, you became a light bearer and a weaver. Your weavings are a joy to behold.

Your passion to awaken others to their souls' wisdom and truth has driven you, and you have not wavered.

We are calling you home to your life in the stars. Your light is needed for a different creation.

Well done, Ashtara Rose. You leave a legacy of love and all you have learned on your journey to the Light. Through your books and the College of Cosmic Consciousness, others can do the same. You light their way.

We eagerly await your return.

***

AFTERWORD

The following is a deeply personal message from Mary, a Magdalen, who explains how she is embodied within Ashtara to guide their shared evolution into greater light. She reveals her past life role in assisting Yeshua (Jesus) and how the Divine Mother Goddess was suppressed for two thousand years. Mary shares insights into her own initiation in the Great Pyramid and her post-crucifixion travels to France and England, affirming her oneness with Ashtara and their joint mission to awaken humanity's ancient wisdom.

***

Mary, a Magdalen speaks:

I Am Mary, a Magdalen, embodied in Ashtara's womb for the purpose of guiding her, and our, evolution into greater light. We know we are of the One Soul, the Divine Mother, birther of all souls.

We are one with All That Is and rejoice in this knowing.

In my life as an Essene and a Magdalen, I incarnated to assist Yeshua/Kuthumi demonstrate to the world his physical ascension from the darkness of matter to the Light of Spirit. His teachings were not understood and became a vehicle of control through dogmatism and erroneous belief. It has been so for two thousand years.

The Divine Mother Goddess was purposefully deleted from all texts to enable a masculine God figure to dominate. And so it has been.

Ashtara remembers much of her life as an aspect of our one soul; however, I am to share with her, and with you, the truth.

I was trained in the pyramids along the Nile and took my final initiation in the sarcophagus of the Great Pyramid, where others of like vibration were also placed to complete their training. Some died, unable to return from the lives they were seemingly living in from the past. Many dark demons of memory emerge when placed in a sarcophagus devoid of light.

Training the mind to focus on the vibration of love is the practice needed to overcome the dark influences.

Yeshua's initiation was public and his symbolic process was to experience a crucifixion of his lower self into the light of the Higher Self. He said that what he did could also be done by others. I chose the sarcophagus for my initiation, as did Ashtara.

She arose, like the phoenix bird, out of the ashes of her former self into the recognition and connection to her soul, our soul. We are One and, as one, we are to spend the rest of Ashtara's remaining life in this state of being.

Ashtara has travelled to my former home and experienced memories. She walked on the sands of Galilee where Yeshua and I walked. She travelled to France to revisit my life there following the crucifixion. No longer could I live in the Holy Land. It was unsafe for me to do so. My father, Joseph of Arimathea, provided a small boat for me, my young daughter Sar'h, and some other Essenes to travel to France. We were safe there for a few years until the Romans invaded. I spent my time there teaching and healing. Also in and around Glastonbury in England, where I spent some years in the area.

Yeshua, in his lighter body, joined us on many occasions. Great celebrations occurred when his presence was known.

Our Essene community rejoined for the last time when a great celebration occurred at Fortingall, Scotland. From there, the seeds of our Light, our consciousness, scattered and are now being awakened in the minds of former Initiates of the Light.

Since my embodiment into Ashtara's womb, she is remembering her soul's history. On her next journey to southern France, Glastonbury and Fortingall, she will remember more. I am with her to share her journey of remembrance.

We are One.

GLOSSARY

Age of Aquarius: The Age of Enlightenment. Relative to the themes of the sign of Aquarius. The Sun's apparent retrograde movement determines an Age through an area of space of a particular constellation, approximately 2,592 Earth years in duration.

Akasha / Akashic Records: A nonphysical repository of all universal knowledge, or a universal energy field of information that includes all human experience. Every human can access their personal Akashic records should they choose to elevate their consciousness sufficiently to do so.

Ascension: Is a step-by-step process that every human Soul takes on its return journey to merge again with Great Spirit/God/Supreme Intelligence – Source of all life. When this takes place is determined by the consciousness level of each incarnated Soul. Ascension from this earthly 3D plane is one step in the process.

Astral plane: This plane of illusion, archetypes, glamour and a distorted representation of reality relates to the emotional plane. There is a lower and higher astral world.

Annunaki: "Anunnaki" translates to "those who came from the heavens," suggesting their origin is not from Earth.

Mission Camelot: A group endeavour initiated by the Arcturians and guided by Ashtara for the intent and purpose of doing whatever is needed to bring about a new Age of Light where harmony, truth, wisdom and beauty are prevalent and dominant in the majority of human minds.

Paneurythmy: A sacred circle dance, gifted to the world last century by Bulgarian Spiritual Master, Beinsa Duono, known also as Peter Deunov. Ashtara travelled to Bulgaria in 1995 to learn this dance because her memories of dancing it in other lives were so strong. From the year 2001 and for nine consecutive she led groups to the sacred sites of Peru and Bolivia to dance Paneurythmy. Through the sacredness of the dance, and the experience of divine love within the hearts of the dancers ancient knowledge chambers were re-activated and many soul memories awakened, not only for Ashtara but also for some of the group dancers. Through specific movements aligned with the beautiful music, the dancers form geometric patterns that connect to the sacred geometry of the cosmos. From 1995 to 2025, Ashtara danced with different groups, awakening their love vibration. Uluru, in the central heart of Australia, was one of the sacred sites visited. At that dance, 250 people joined her from around the world.

Prime Creator's Plan: A process whereby the soul descends into the lower vibrational frequencies of matter to experience life eventually returning to again unite within the great hologram of Prime Creator's Love. Vast experience and knowledge is gained through the process. We humans are amazing creators.

Rainbow Serpent: An archetypal figure described in Australian Aboriginal stories as the birther of all souls and the ultimate creator. The author describes, in her book A Story Never Ever Told, A REVEAL, an intense experience at Uluru, the sacred monolith and solar plexus chakra of our planet, where she felt herself to be the Rainbow Serpent, giving birth to thousands of human souls...

Rainbow Warriors of Peace / Light: The name given by the Arcturians to the new souls being birthed with a higher level of consciousness to that of the majority of humans on planet Earth. They are birthing in their thousands now, often as autists. They are our future. They need us to raise our consciousness levels through greater self-awareness so we can assist them and make their mission for incarnation ours. Love is the key.

Sedna: A dwarf planet approaching Earth for the first time in thousands of years. Sedna's archetypal energy acts as a messenger and her approach is linked to potential planetary upheaval and frequency shifts on Earth. Identified with the planet Nibiru from Sumerian texts, the beings from this planet are called the Annunaki.

Seven Rays of Creation: In the beginning, the one Source of all Light and Love chose to experience different aspects of Itself. In order to do so, separation was needed. Through a cosmic prism, seven entities were created - each with a different vibration and colour. The energy content of these entities is so vast it travels to all areas of Creation, infusing it with Prime Creator's Love and Light. These Rays are manifestations of Prime Creator/God. They influence all living things. The way they do so is part of the Great Mysteries, known as esoteric science that involves astrology.

Shadow Psychology: Dark selfish thoughts, deeds and actions. Human psychology devoid of light and the recognition and acceptance of Prime Creator's love.

Spiritual Science: Behind all creation is a spiritual science, known as the Divine Plan for the evolution of the human soul. It is the science of energy. The Seven Rays of Creation form an important part of this science.

Star of David Formation: A configuration of geometry when two equilateral triangles intersect, forming one shape.

Telepathy: A natural ability all human beings were gifted with when first created as independent souls. This ability, like others, can atrophy through lack of self-awareness and use. It is a communication method that will be a valuable resource in times to come. Reflect on power outages. How can you contact your loved ones when there is no power to do so? It's wise indeed to develop your telepathy. Love is the key.

Uluru: A giant monolith in the centre of Australia. It is identified as one of Earth's chakras, specifically the solar plexus or navel of the Earth. It is a birthing place, a library of ancient wisdom and knowledge, constructed by advanced space technology. It was the site of a global activation and the birthing of a new Light on January 30th, 2025.

Zodiac: The Earth receives specific radiation from twelve constellations of stars. Taken together, these constellations surround the earth like a wheel. We call this huge wheel the "zodiac". What are these radiations and how can we use them constructively? Through learning about and consciously utilising their different energies. This practice is known as the ancient science of esoteric astrology.

For more definitions, visit www.ashtara.com

**

Ashtara is an astrologer, spiritual teacher of the esoteric mysteries, scribe and messenger for cosmic sources. A consciousness pioneer, she has shared her wisdom and soul guidance for over 30 years. Known for her clarity, humility, and telepathic connection with higher-dimensional beings, Ashtara has dedicated her life to raising human consciousness and restoring the Light of truth.

You can reach her via her website www.ashtara.com

Your Notes

Your Notes

www.ingramcontent.com/pod-product-compliance
Lightning Source LLC
Chambersburg PA
CBHW031425290426
44110CB00011B/527